Esparienna

TALES OF AN ISLAND WOMAN

Darnnalee Gilbert

♥

Published by Darnnalee Gilbert

Copyright © 2020. All rights reserved. No portion of this publication may be used, reproduced or transmitted by any means, digital, electronic, mechanical, photocopy or recording without written permission of the publisher, except in the case of brief quotations within critical articles or reviews.

ISBN: 978-0-646-82076-7 (paperback)

For book orders and enquiries contact:
avalonstar25fire@outlook.com

DEDICATION

To my Mother with loving memories,
love and peace.

CONTENTS

Preface vii
I am no hero; just an ordinary woman 1
Father 2
War is here 3
Influence by friends 4
The elements 5
You are a beautiful person 6
Inspiration from the cloud 7
Forgotten days 8
She is so beautiful 9
Time goes swiftly 10
Bang, bang, baby 11
If you lose me 12
Man in my head 13
You text others not me 14
Mind of a toy 15
Brown eyed boy 16
Questions, questions 17
Looking for my past 18
Used 19
Sharday, sharday 20
The blessed 21
I am ESPARIENNA 22
Sweet to know 23
Forbidden love 24
Love under the palm tree 25
Down by the sea 26
Can you admit it? 27
Who are you? 28
When I'm with you 29
Picture on the wall 30
I'm drifting away 31
Rise with darkness 32

If you are not true to her	33
Missing you sick	34
Voice of a man	35
Doubts	36
Hello water from fire	37
Stand by each other	38
Piece of land	39
Together we are one	40
My curious fool	41
I had a dream	42
Mindful	43
Love is a beautiful thing	44
Another land	45
A question of God	46
Crazy mystical	47
If I try my hardest	48
Hear my voice	49
The rain	50
Dream wondering mind	51
The eyes of an eagle	52
He caught my attention	53
The innocents	54
Darkness inside me	55
Things on my mind	56
Sweet love	57
I see you in my dreams	58
Has your perception of me changed?	59
Is my child not my child?	60
The wind	61
Aftermath	62
Friends	63
Vengeance!	64
Forgiveness	65
You're hovering!	66
Confusion	67
Sprite of my life	68
Have a little faith	69
Stop blinding your eyes from me	70

PREFACE

During my life, I have successfully raised three children and put myself through college and many short courses to further my education. Helping and counselling others became my career.

Having experienced the highs and lows of life: love, marriage, divorce and disappointments, I saw how far I and others have come. The inner person inside of me started putting words on paper. Often I would throw them away until one day someone read my poems and suggested I write a book.

When I first started writing, I never imagined that I would reach this point. I'd like to thank this special person, who will never leave my heart.

I give thanks to my children, grandchildren, family members, friends and Rommie from Hardshell Publishing who helped guide me through the process of becoming a published author. The one who gave me the most inspiration to write is our creator, God, who opened and exposed my mind, giving me the inspiration to write this book and have it published.

May you enjoy reading these poems as much as I have enjoyed writing them.

Darnnalee Gilbert

I AM NO HERO; JUST AN ORDINARY WOMAN

I am no Hero; I am just an Ordinary Woman.
I have a broken heart,
the scars you see on my body
are not anything as bad as the ones inside me,
I have been hurt by what I had thought to be true love,
over and over again.

I am no Hero; I am just an Ordinary Woman.
I have been burnt, I have been raped,
I have been kicked down to the floor,
and when I got back up,
I was slapped back down to the ground again.

Don't look at me this way, like you are ashamed of me.
Don't talk to me this way, like you pity me
and I'm a fool to stay with him.
I have learned the hard way,
I am no Hero; I am just an Ordinary Woman.

You think you know it all, don't you?
'Leave him' you all say,
easier said than done.
He brings me flowers, and little trinkets to please me,
he tells me he loves me,
he's only protecting me from all the shit out there in the world.

A day or two later he knocks me down,
to the floor again.
I have learned the hard way,
I have learned now, enough,
and no more.
My time has come I've had enough.

I am no Hero; I am just an Ordinary Woman.
But, I have taken control of my life now,
left my bags behind, no need to take the past with me.
My mind and body is free, I am free now.

I am still no Hero;
But I am a Woman!

FATHER

You're the best Father,
the very best.

Thank you for being
like the air we breathe in and out,
it shows you care, Father.

There is always love in your eyes,
with so much concern for others.
Thank you for caring, in so many ways, Father.

You're the crust of my eyes.
As the crust that holds the bread together,
so do you hold us, our family together.

You walk tall, even on the worst of your days.
Your hands are rough and worn, you tell us
they're hands of a working man, with a smile on your face.
Your black hair with flecks of grey is always neat and tidy.

Your taste for life Father, has no taste,
but to be natural and fresh,
with the sweet smelling of love.

You are my Father,
you are my best friend,
I am your Beloved, we are as one.

WAR IS HERE

My heart is beating 100 beats per minute,
the ache is finally here,
It's like a storm, WAR is here.

There are many homicidal, suicidal, maniacs here,
we can see them all.
We can see through their lies
and their false smiles.
They have brought with them WAR,
pestilence and disease.
We have never seen the likes of before now.

Doctors and scientists,
sorry you will not find the cure this time.
You are the ones that have designed this disease,
this pestilence, with no name but WAR.

It breaks my heart as it beats 100 beats per minute,
to see all these well-educated men and women destroy everything.
They said it was the best thing they have ever done,
designing a cure for the world, they tell us.

They thought they were making a better world,
but they didn't realise they were destroying this world,
they were inventing WAR.
Designing and making their bombs, nuclear weapons
to fight against each other.

Yes, there are many homicidal, suicidal, maniacs here,
we can see them.
We can see through their lies and their false smiles,
they have brought with them WAR,
pestilence of disease.
We have never seen the likes of before now.

But only the innocent will be suffering,
while the man that signed the papers starts the WAR!
Then hides in that well planned, built safe house.
Our flesh burns to the bones while he hides.
WAR IS HERE.

INFLUENCE BY FRIENDS

If you've come all this way and did not come to see us,
then something must be wrong.
I know some friends can influence each other.

When some friends fall in love and the other is out of love,
they don't want you to be in love,
they want you to roll with them.

Messages on the internet teaching couples how to treat one another,
what to say to each other,
how to text each other,
how to let the other one wait and beg for your attention.
Load of rubbish.
Your just being influenced by others!

If you love somebody, tell them how you feel.
Don't be afraid to be in their face, with your feelings.
Let them know it is them that you truly love.
That's the way we should all roll, don't be controlled by others.

What's so wrong in putting your feelings on the table out there?
Express yourself!
If it's not right for the one you tell, your heart will get broken,
why delay the pain that is going to happen in any case.
It's over and done with.
Do not be arseholes, say what you have got to say!

Don't be influenced by your friends, be upfront, say it.
If you diddle around stretching it out,
the pain is only going to be worse, when the let down comes.
But, at least this way, you've said what you had to say.

Let the other person deal with it, let them have their say,
don't be influenced by your friends.
Move on with life together or not together,
don't let it be because you were influenced by your friends.
You could regret it someday.

Tell your friends, Butt out!
Let you make your own mistakes.

THE ELEMENTS

From the North, the South,
the East, and the West.

I can hear the element of the Wind roaring,
the feel of the Air gathering around me.

Beneath my feet I feel the Earth element trembling,
above my head I see the trees wrestling with the Air,
Water falls from Heaven, bless us all.

Far out at sea the element of Water races like wild horses.
Building up its waves as it reaches the shore,
it crashes against the rocks with a cry of a mighty power.

Oh element of Fire, Fire straight and bright across the sky,
you shine with glory burning brimstones,
showering across the Earth.

My head swells with fear,
But! yet my body stands content with looking on.
Only to realise,
the four elements have come together
within the four corners of the Earth.

They have come to hear my crying,
as I've being longing and waiting for so long
to see their gathering,
to feel the power of the elements,
feeling the wind guiding them to me.
Oh what glorious power and feeling it is.

From the North, the South,
the East and the West,
the elements came together for me.

YOU ARE A BEAUTIFUL PERSON

You are a beautiful person,
your smile shines.
You light up every pathway you walk down.
Your eyes are as bright as stars,
they show and say you're a beautiful person.

There is much, much more beauty inside of you,
more than any person can ever see.
Your heart is always giving, yet very rarely
do we ever see you take from anyone.

Let them all talk, let them all laugh,
you are a beautiful person.
It is because they have no confidence
In themselves, why they speak uncomfortable things
about you.
It is because they cannot find
beauty in themselves.

They smear and tease you,
pay no attention, jealousy is their weapon.
Do not cry, wipe your tears.
You are a beautiful person
Inside and outside.

The universe has its arms wrapped around you,
stay strong.

INSPIRATION FROM THE CLOUD

Sometimes I get my inspiration from the clouds.
Some people say I have a wild imagination.
I must admit I sometimes do see many pathways
through the clouds.

I wondered what would have happened
if I had stopped that child and talked to her face-to-face,
she looked so sad, her mind seemed so far away.
She could have made it rain with that sad face,
if only she knew, she had the power inside of her,
the kind of power to make it rain,
or bring the sunshine out, and brighten up the day.
But I did not stop her.

Now I have another chance!
I was standing around gazing up to the clouds
before I saw this child walking along.
I wondered what it meant earlier,
seeing the shape of a child in the clouds.
What will today bring?
But, I was mortified by the sadness of the face
in the cloud earlier,
I thought no more of it,
until I saw that child walk on by.

I looked again and wondered.
It was then the cloud came back into my
thoughts, the shape of a child standing alone,
I must speak to this child, so I did,
and grateful for doing so,
as I saw myself in this child's actions.

It was at that time again my mind rushed
back through to the cloud, and its pathway.
What it meant for me, was to help a child, a stranger.

But not so strange, that I could not see myself, my past
in this child. Because I did, thanks to the inspiration
from the cloud.

FORGOTTEN DAYS

Today has gone past so quickly,
like the breeze passing through my hair,
as I sit here looking through my window.
Visions of my thoughts passing through my mind,
of forgotten days.

Yet! I cannot help thinking of you
and wondering why you hurt me so.
I trust in you young love,
you tried so hard at first to get my love,
I tried so hard just to be a friend to you.

I gave in and you trapped me
like an insect in a web.
Now I am waiting for the spinner
to take me out of this web.
So tomorrow I can sit at my window again
and smile at forgotten days.

Standing on my own foundation
I am going to be stronger.
Be stronger than the day I met you,
I am ready.

I am going to refuse you young love,
oh you're just a boy in a man's body.
You are not mature yet, for a woman like me.
I am a woman too mature for a boy like you,
leave me alone, let me think.

This must be like a day gone quickly,
like the breeze passing through my hair
as I sit here looking through my window.

I promise I will never trust in young love again.
You can't help the way you are my young love,
so please let me forget you,
like the breeze passing through,
passing through my hair, let this be a forgotten day.

SHE IS SO BEAUTIFUL

From the first moment I saw her
tears flooded my eyes.

She is so beautiful,
I admired her perfection.
Her eyes like the stars in the sky at night,
just as the darkness appears and the first blink
of the first starlight shines.

She is so beautiful,
her skin so soft,
her hair so fine,
the looks upon her lips are priceless.

Nine months of waiting.
Oh I thank the almighty,
she is here safely.
I cannot say if she is smiling or yawning
or just a combination of
Eyes, Nose, Cheeks and Mouth,
all moving at once, saying
hello, I am here at last.

She is so beautiful.
her five fingers on each hand,
her five toes on each foot
makes her perfect,
already she makes me feel so proud.

She is so beautiful.
I would love her in any way or form
that she had come to me because she is mine.
She is so beautiful.

TIME GOES SWIFTLY

My oh my, how time goes by so swiftly.
It seems like only yesterday, a short time ago
since they came into this world.

I remember so clearly the first tooth,
the first word, the first step.
Time goes so swiftly.

Tippy toes, off they go
the soft lightly steps,
no noise just sounds like whispers,
drifting away down the hallway.

How did it get this way?
Footsteps that rustle away
down the hallway,
not towards me.
But away from me,
oh, time goes so swiftly.

Sounds of tipping toes moving further
away from my ears, off they go again,
teenage years.

Again, no one knows where they're going,
out the door, they're gone to be with their peers.

Let us make our own mistakes, they say.
That is how we will learn, they tell me.
But I'm petrified for them.
As they walk out that door my thoughts are?
Time goes so swiftly.

BANG, BANG, BABY

Bang, bang baby. You dropped.
I told your sister it wasn't I that did it.
I told your brother, I never rolled over
and stumbled all over you.

Your mama came around to my house, horrified she was.
Bang, bang, bang you dropped baby, I never did it.
Everyone looked to you to save me, but I have to save myself.
The crowd came in, they pushed me to the side.
I fell to the ground, I heard the noise bang, bang.

Baby, you dropped to the ground, right on top of me.
I didn't do it, I told the policeman,
I told the detective, I did not detect you coming,
I did not detect the crowd today.

But you came in force and the crowd surrounded you.
You were the king of this street at one time,
you were the music of this street.

Baby, you're still the voice of this street.
When the crowd see you, they surround you,
but, bang, bang, this time you dropped to the ground
and no one knows who pulled the trigger.

Is this the respect you told me of these people?
They respect you so much, you told me,
these people love you so much.
Is this the way they show their love
to their king of the street,
to their street master, with a bang, bang.
Baby, you dropped to the ground
right on top of me, you fell.

I saved your ass from dying,
bang, bang baby, show me you were worth it.
Show me some respect.

IF YOU LOSE ME

If you walk out the door and leave right now,
you are going to lose me.

And if you lose me, you will lose a good person.
If you leave right now,
don't look back, don't come back,
I won't be waiting!!

I won't be standing at the door
holding it for you to walk back in,
oh no baby I've given you the best of my days,
the best of my nights and life.

I've been like a slave to you;
you've been nothing like that to me.
You always think you're above me,
but if we're not equal then you're nothing to me,
and I am nothing to you,
If you lose me! You lose the best part of yourself.

The days of master and being your mistress are over for me,
you're either standing by my side,
or you're standing behind me,
but never again in front of me.

I know my path, I will take it alone.
I've been there helping you up every time you fall.
But if you should lose me now,
you will lose the best thing that's ever happened to you.
No mistake.

MAN IN MY HEAD

Comfort does not lie beneath my skin anymore.
I lost respect of my own by putting you first,
so many times when you did not deserve me.
Man in my head,
I let you rule my mind over and over again.

My sins haunt me night and day,
I cannot be in love this way.
My feelings,
my head is spinning,
no sleep,
just thinking all the time
sending me crazy,
I wish I had a motive to get these
thoughts out of my head,
too many doubts,
too many suspicions.

Stupid choices I have made, have bought
hurricane and thunderstorms in my life.
No more hiding and shutting in my thoughts,
and feelings no, no more.

Man in my head,
no more tap dancing around my thoughts,
I am going to play my favourite song,
dance like crazy to find my comfort
beneath my skin.

It is raining outside,
man in my head, I respect you.
Do you respect me enough?
to come dancing with me?

Look, a rainbow,
let us find comfort together in each other arms,
let comfort crawl beneath our skin,
once more together,
Man in my head.

YOU TEXT OTHERS NOT ME

The thought of you,
ringing someone else and not me.
The thought of you,
texting someone else and not me.

Only makes you a disloyal person,
the thought of you lying to me
makes me sick.

Here I am waiting to hear from you patiently,
there you are texting, talking to strangers
on your phone again.

Texting strangers on your phone,
accepting strangers on your phone,
but yet you have no time for me.
To call me or text me.

Not even just to say
"hi, how are you?"
I'm committed to you,
you tell me you're committed to me.

But you know nothing of loyalty, commitment, trust
you have no dignity,
you ghost me online, while your texting others,
you leave me hanging on like a piece of string.

You tell me you love me, you miss me,
you need me, you want me,
what is love to you?
Love is just a word to you;
love is a word you use to keep me hanging on to you.

Texting strangers on your phone,
accepting strangers on your phone.
To you, "Love is like the belt holding your trousers up
one day they'll break and love will fall far from you."

MIND OF A TOY

My oh my,
My master has come at last,
to comfort my mistress with his love.

Tonight I am not needed to comfort my mistress.
I lay here on my mistress bed for days and nights,
while she waits for my master's arms around her body.

Every night she takes me to bed with her, and holds me tight,
she thinks of me as her best friend in the world,
my mistress talks to me, she tells me her most hurtful feelings.
My mistress hurts for the love of my master, in his absence,
every morning she rises and reaches out for me next to her.

Some nights she reads her favourite book,
but always she talks to me in her bed,
In the mornings she might read to me the notes from my master.

Tonight my mistress' eyes
her body, her heart and soul is only for my master.
My mistress' lover, my master is here with her tonight,
but tomorrow he will be gone again,
leaving her filled with his love.

I know the love my mistress carries for my master
will always be there in her heart.
My thoughts are that my mistress
does not need or want no other
but my master,
she prays for the love of the angels, to come take her away,
if she cannot be loved by my master,
If my master should ever turn away from my mistress,
she wishes that her last breath to be taken from her.

Love from your servant Frog.

BROWN EYED BOY

Hey, brown eyed boy, you look good in your white shirt,
and your blue trousers tonight.
Did I tell you how you moved your groove so sexy and smooth,
when you walked across the road coming towards me?
I watched the way your hips move in your blue jeans,
I imagined your hips, my hips, close up rubbing together, oh boy.

Your stride moves with sex written all over you, just like a panther
slowly hunting, (his muscles expand as he moves faster to his prey)
so does yours! through your blue jeans coming towards me.
Brown eyed boy, did I tell you, you look real delicious in those
blue trousers? I want to take them off you. I like the way they
wrap around your body, I want to see what's underneath them,
I'm curious...

I love the way you move in your white shirt, you move like a
panther, fit and healthy sleek coming towards me with your
shirt unbuttoned revealing your tight fit brown chest.
Slowly you move towards me.
You see me standing waiting for you, I look you up and down.
I see myself naked, swimming around in a pool of chocolate
through the vision of your brown eyes.
I'm waiting for you to lick me all over, oh my!
I have no control over my body when I'm around you, delicious.
Boy your skin looks so smooth, you look like a cup of coffee,
with just a little bit of milk added.

Boy, oh boy, whoop, whoop, ching, ching, cha-cha.
I'll make your dreams come true,
whip cream all over your brown body. What follows next?
Use your imagination baby, meet me in the foyer.
Brown eyed boy in your white shirt
and your blue trousers, you look so sexy, like a panther breathing
steadily over its prey after catching it before indulging.
That will be, you and I tonight.
I'm coming your way, wait for me.
I'm going to make your dreams come true tonight,
brown eyed boy in that white shirt
and blue trousers, hmmm.

QUESTIONS, QUESTIONS

Why do you never say you need me?

Why should I go so far to prove myself worthy of you,
or anyone else?

Why can I not just be me?

Why do you disapprove of me as I am,
yet you say you want to be with me?

Why can you not say the words "I LOVE YOU"?

Why do you show me love yet not say it?

Why is your heart so two sided?

Why are you here one minute and gone the next?

Why, where do you go?

Why do I love you so much?

Why do I never get the right answers from you?

Why do you lie to me for no reason?

Why do you expect me to understand,
when you don't understand me?

Why do you want to throw your life away?
Being with someone you don't want to be with most of the time?

Answer me?
You are a person who is afraid of commitment to love... W-H-Y

LOOKING FOR MY PAST

I need to know about my past,
I have no time to talk,
I have got to keep on walking,
I have found a number,
but I have no understanding of it.

This cannot wait,
where can I find the mystery of my past?
Every time I turn around
everything seems disabled.

My mind is like a spell, has been cast over me.

I am a victim,
I am linked with my past.
I need to know about my past now
I am trying my hardest
to keep my mind focused on the future.

Many times I have been influenced,
Got side tracked by my mind.
If I could find an informer
with the information I need,
then my future would focus clearly.
I could be bold enough to take my past.

I would close my eyes, think brave reach out
and grab my past,
so to pave the way for my future.
Take it and run with it.

USED

I am here waiting for you,
like a used book on a shelf, waiting to be read.

I count the minutes, days and weeks
and now you come back to me.

You just walk right back through my door
and I accept you,
and you expect it from me.
We go right into making love day in days out.

You know I have not been doing anything wrong,
so you ask no questions of me,
just like a used book, you turn the pages to where you left it,
you start touching me, and you put a smile
right back on my face, seeing you feeling you.

You hold me in your arms like your old cup fill with warm coffee
and squeeze me real tight,
you do the things to me that make me
forget you were ever gone.

We make love, days in days out.
Six months later you're gone again.

What is going on? I ask myself.
What is wrong with this picture?

This I must not accept,
I cannot accept it any longer
This, you cannot expect of me no more.
I am used up.

SHARDAY, SHARDAY

Sharday, show me what you want from me.
Show me what you need,
show me your mind Sharday.

Let me see inside of you,
let me try and help you,
show me Sharday.
Let me look inside
let me see what I can see.

You're so troubled, my child,
I wish I could help you,
I wish I could hold you.

You're so far away, far away,
the other side of the world Sharday.
Let me see inside of you,
let me look inside of you Sharday.

Sharday rain is coming,
I can smell it in the air.
I know if you show me your troubles,
I will ask the rain to wash them away today.

I will ask the rain to wash your troubles away.
Just show me what you need to show me,
let me inside your mind,
so I can see your troubled soul, Sharday.

Let me look inside of you,
let me see what I can see.
Sharday, Sharday,
come now stand beside me,
let the rain wash away your troubles.

My beloved, it is the Angles crying for you Sharday,
their tears are washing your troubles away.
Sharday, Sharday.

THE BLESSED

God bless those who see the needy
and reaches out to them,
with love and gracefulness.
The Sky is the limit for some.

Rewards of charity is theirs,
not on Earth but in Heaven.
Some can afford to visit the moon.
But so many of us seem to think we can
go further beyond the sky.

Only a month ago, I read,
a woman said her husband bought her
a star, and name it after her.
What's next I thought, are they the blessed ones?

We see, what we want to see,
but do we really know what it is
that we are really looking for.
I wonder if the sky is the limit,
after all for any of us?

You can win all the lottery money in this world
and help your family and friends.
But please don't forget the needy.
Give a little with gratitude;
bless them with love and kindness.

As you may not know, this has come to you as a test.
God bless those who see the needy,
and reaches out to them, the blessed.

I AM ESPARIENNA

When the darkness comes around,
you will not be afraid anymore
now that I am with you.

Oh no, you won't be afraid anymore,
now that I have learned how to call upon the universe.
Nature has taught me the way.
If you look you shall find me.
If you reach out your hands far enough you shall touch me.
In the morning, afternoon, evening and the nights,
my spirit never sleeps.
Feel the wind upon your cheeks; it is I that kisses you.
Whenever you wish for me.
If you wish hard enough I shall be there for you.

Just call my name ESPARIENNA
Just call my name ESPARIENNA
ESPARIENNA I am.

I have many names but this one is just for you.
This name is a name of magic and inspiration.

I am the mystical fire that keeps you warm day through to night,
I am the mystical wind that wraps my arms around you
and whispers in your ears, confidence, strength,
and encourages you along those hard moments in your life.
I am the mystical water that quenches your thirst
and rolls off your body at nights.
When you sweat in your sleep,
it is I that is holding onto you so tight,
keeping you safe in your dream state.
I am the mystical earth that grounds you,
and keeps you safe and balanced at all times.

Don't be afraid! Do not hesitate!
Just call my name ESPARIENNA
Just call my name ESPARIENNA
I am ESPARIENNA watching over you!

SWEET TO KNOW

So you're still thinking of me
at this precious moment in life?
Sweet to know.

The lord is about to destroy the earth
and you're singing a song about me.
Lenders, borrowers, buyers, sellers,
tomorrow all your wealth will mean nothing no more.
The Earth will mourn us all.

The wonderful sounds of trumpets from heaven,
will play their sweet music.
While fires falling from the sky,
I will still be known as fire as I am.

Light is my path and white is my way,
show me the rainbow and I will take it and follow it.
It's sweet to know, you're still thinking of me
at this precious moment in life.

Night after night I have remained faithful to you.
My stomach aches and burns with pain, like a woman in labour.
I lay here wondering and asking myself
if you still remember me.
I was wondering if you're really thinking of me.

But it is sweet to know your still thinking of me!
I will not break my everlasting covenant of celibate.
I will stay faithful till we meet again.
I have always known this day would come.

The world to an end and you're still thinking of me
at this precious moment in life.
The lord is about to destroy the earth
and you're singing a song about me.
Lenders, borrowers, buyers, sellers,
tomorrow all your wealth will mean nothing no more.
The Earth will mourn us all, but you, you're still thinking of me
at this precious moment in life.

FORBIDDEN LOVE

I have never touched you.
I have never kissed you.
I have never stroked your face.
I have never embraced your body.

All I have ever done is look upon you, with thoughts
of no thoughts at all.
But yet when you spoke a few words to me,
and I back to you, life changed.
Forbidden love knows no boundary.

I stood afar and gazed upon you,
like a fairytale.
I walked past you, you saw me, and you looked at me,
as I walked on by.
I turned my head over my right shoulder and gazed upon you.

As I move slowly past you, I wanted to run back
and place my lips upon yours,
and whisper in your ears, how much I want you.
I was afraid it was forbidden.
Even though forbidden love knows no boundary.

But yet still I felt it was forbidden to do so
and kept on walking,
I am so much in love with you.
Yet I have never touched you.
I have never kissed you.
You have never touched me or kissed me.
My heart aches,
My belly aches,
I am dying inside for you.
Forbidden Love.

LOVE UNDER THE PALM TREE

Remember how we used to sit by this memorising beach?
Underneath that palm tree,
once a month we would do this,
we would call it an evening and a night to remember.

Remember how I use to lay my head in your lap?
While you read to me under that palm tree,
and when the sun was going down
we used to lay and watch it as it goes down.

We would say, "a kiss for the sunset"
then our hands would reach out,
together our fingertips would touch
and we would point them to the sunset as it goes down.

When the sun is gone we would take our hands and
gently rub them over each other's face.
I would always let my fingertips rub over your forehead,
down your nose, then over the shape of your lips
and you would do the same to me, and then we would kiss.

We would gently whisper in each other's ears saying "it's time"
we would look for those beautiful memories
In each other eyes for just a little while longer.

Then we would smile at each other,
we would make love to each other, underneath
that palm tree, on this beach, as the sunsets.
Here we are now, years have gone by, and we are still
In love with each other, and young in our hearts
Walking towards that very same palm tree.

DOWN BY THE SEA

It is so peaceful here.
I know I should be going,
but somehow I feel I should stay
for a while longer.

My mind feels free of problems down here by the sea,
the sun shines down glittering across the sea.
It shines down and embraces the sea,
the silvery reflection bounces off the surface
with warm air, a feeling of peace.
Here down by the sea,
my mind is at rest.

The sound of the waves beating against the rocks,
the crashing sounds of comfort,
as the waves make their way through the rocks.

The birds overhead are anxious
with aggressiveness in their sounds,
as they fly downwards to the seashore,
looking and searching for their next meal.

People drive into the lookout, stopping parking and,
some stay for a while gazing at the water,
Yet some just drive around and away they go again.

As for me, I wonder how many drops of water are there
in one of those big waves, splashing and crashing
against the rocks over there?

Down by the sea,
It is beautiful; I am so much at peace here,
down by the sea.

CAN YOU ADMIT IT?

Can you admit to everything you say?
You say them with a thoughtful thought.
That is why you could never tell me that you love me,
deep down inside you, I know that you love me.

The way that you hold me, the way that you talk to me,
the way we do together the things we do.
Two people just have to have that same kind of love
to share with each other, or am I just dreaming.

Has love lost its meaning in this world?
Or maybe there are just too many people out there
giving it so freely.
Maybe there are just too many people taking love for granted.
Understand me when I say everything you say,
you say it with a thoughtful thought.
That is why you cannot admit you love me.

You are so afraid of hurting me,
you are so afraid of hurting yourself.
But deep down inside of you
I know you love me, can you admit it?
You have been hurt before,
now you're holding back.
You are protecting yourself,
you cannot see what is holding you back,
so why don't you just tell me your feelings?

Can you admit it?
A woman needs to know,
a woman needs to hear it said to her.
Some say "tell me lies, and I will be satisfied"
some say "tell me sweet things, whisper in my ears, I want you"

All I ask of you is the truth.
All I want to hear my love is the truth, from your heart.
I thank God for knowing you.
We have seen each other through some bad times
and still, we are here together.

WHO ARE YOU?

I'm a mystical person, who cares about people and their beliefs.
My passion is for many things in this life.
Yes, I know there is only so much
one can challenge and achieve in one's lifetime,
so I asked you" Who are you"?

Will you come and ride with me?
Come take this mystical train with me,
let's see where it takes us.
The sky is bright and blue, striking red flashes through,
It is my signature of who I am.

My time on this planet is far and few,
I'm from another world as you have learned.
I have been seeking you for many moons now,
and now I have found you.

But it is almost time for me
to return back to my home place. Who are you? You ask,
I seek you and found you, my hunting is over.
My heart desires my home once more,
but only will it survive, with you by my side.

So now will you take this mystical train ride with me?
Or stay here. Will you be my remedy? My medicine of love!
If I stay, I will surely fade away,
If you come with me, you would surely live forever and forever.

Who are you?
I am you, you are me, and we are as one,
I will surely die in your arms;
this can be our mystical train ride home.
Or this can be my mystical train back home, alone.
Who are you? You are my only!

Don't miss this ride, don't worry.
The seasons on earth are falling apart.
It is over for us here, a new beginning for us, on this mystical train ride, back to my home, our home.

WHEN I'M WITH YOU

When I'm with you, I cannot hold back my
feelings for you, you are my poison.
When you're gone I practice over and over,
how to say goodbye to you next time I see you.

Then you come right over, knock at my door, I open it.
All out the door gone my practice of goodbye,
my eyes only see you, my regrets out the window,
I cannot hold back my feelings when I'm with you.

You touch me, and that's all it takes for me to forget
how long it's been since I last saw you,
Inside of my body, I'm tingling all over.

I tell myself how much
I miss your face,
I miss your touch,
I missed your taste,
I just cannot hold back my feelings for you.

When I'm with you, and you look me in my eyes and then
place that moist wet kiss on my lips
so tight I can hardly breathe.
We move backwards slowly close and closer to the bed,
I fall back unto the bed
you fall on top of me, and then...

Heaven opens up,
raining outside, wind blasting up against the window
and we are making love again.
When I'm with you I cannot hold back my feelings for you,
You are my poison.

PICTURE ON THE WALL

Talk to me,
talk to me Picture on the wall.
Tell me your darkest secrets?
Some say they would love to be a fly on the wall,
but I say talk to me,
talk to me picture on the wall, tell me what you know?

I know he has been here,
I know he stayed for a while,
but what I cannot understand is who,
did he stay here with?

Oh, I'm so restless to know the truth.

Talk to me, talk to me.
Talk to me picture on the wall,
tell me what you know!

I bet you know so many things that I am longing to hear.
Why are you sparing my feelings?
I don't want you to hold back.

Oh, picture on the wall,
please, please talk to me.
Tell me all that you know about the man
that stays in this room and his darkest secrets.

Talk to me, talk to me picture on the wall
tell me what you know!

I'M DRIFTING AWAY

I know not where I'm going,
but I hope there will be some familiar faces
where I am heading.

It would be nice to see a pint waiting for me,
with smiles and laughter on faces greeting me.
I once had a pet,
he's been gone, well before me now.

I wonder if he will be there to greet me.
This journey feels very light,
no baggage to carry.

I hope there will be plenty of laughter
where I'm going.
Cheers to you all...

Laughing, singing and memorizing
I leave for you all.
So please, shed no tears.

Remember even in pain
laughter is the remedy for life and healing,
so I say ciao for now see you all later,
my alligators.

RISE WITH DARKNESS

When I rise it shall be with perseverance,
a shimmery glare of light behind the darkness,
you shall see of me.

You shall not recognise me,
the glare of light that I shall rise with will be dim,
but the darkness will blind you with confusion,
it will not last for long,
as you stare me in my face, only darkness you shall see.

I shall rise with darkness inside of me.
You will not be worthy to look me in my eyes no more.
Weakness shall not know me no more,
strength, I will rise with and bear within me.

Those that have deceived me must be removed from my new path.
Love! This light is gone from me,
so I may take my revenge.
Darkness will walk by my side for a while.

It's not what I have been searching for,
but that is what I will be given to rise with,
my enemies have made this of me.
I will shut them down,
stamp them out, and then go back
to receive my light of halo, so I may rise once again
with the light burning inside of me,
hovering around and above me.

I will return more glorious than I was!
You shall not recognize me when I return once again.
My glare of light that I will rise with,
shall blind you all,
If you dare to look upon me, with dishonesty towards me,
you shall not be worthy of me no more.

Knowing darkness will be left behind,
I will only carry inside of me
the light of worthiness.

IF YOU ARE NOT TRUE TO HER

Over many years,
her body has been her Temple.
After men have broken and torn her down to the ground.
No man has been worthy to enter her temple since.

GOD, ALLAH and all other names known as,
has made sure no man on this earth defiled her temple again.

Are you ready for that long journey with her?
Do you think that you are worthy to enter her temple?
Be aware, she is fire.
Should you defile her temple with lies and deceitfulness?
GOD, ALLAH and all other names known as,
will burn your soul with the flames that are not Eternal fire
but suffering!

Are you ready to make her your princess?
and she makes you her prince?
He who dares to say yes and be true to her,
GOD your GOD will and shall reward you both, with
the life that you both have been searching for.

As long as you respect and love each other, be truthful
to one another, never leave each other
when the rough times come.

Be always there to see each other through them
and come out stronger together.
GREAT GOD, ALLAH and all other names known as
will be there at the end to greet you.

MISSING YOU SICK

When my body was running at a temperature of 39.5,
I was burning up.
When I woke up out of my bed and my clothes were so wet,
they felt like I had just taken them out of the washing machine,
without spinning the water out of them.
My body was aching so much, my head was spinning,
missing you sick.
The days seem like nights, and the nights seem like days,
I wish that I could have reached of out to you,
next to me, to hold me tight,
comfort me in this time that I felt so needy, missing you sick.

In this moment of time, I certainly felt where is love?
I could not stand up, I felt like I was at sea, standing in the
smallest of boats in the roughest of waters around me.
My room spinning as my thoughts work their way towards you,
but I could not call you, I could not send a message to you.
Because you wanted me, to let you miss me, and I to miss you.

Well, let me tell you something.
I miss you every single day and night.
You're the first thing and the last thing that I think of
day and night. If you don't feel the same way about me,
there's no need for me and you to carry on.

The time that I needed you most was that time,
I could not have picked up a phone and call you,
because, I did not want to bother you.
Was this enough for you to miss me? Me missing you sick!
Well if that's what it takes for you to miss me,
then, I wish you were there when I was so sick,
burning up at a temperature of 39.5.
I did not need to miss you, or for you to miss me.
I only needed you to lay by my side, and hold on to me.

That's not love, that's just you, somebody who wants to be there,
when it suits you, not when someone needs you,
when it suits you, and only then.

VOICE OF A MAN

You walked up to me like an Angel in a dream,
you smiled at me,
you sprayed your essence of perfume around me,
filled with emptiness inside of me, I heard the voice of a man
I then looked up at you and saw your face,
you said something sweet from your lips,
I remembered,
your words sounded like a violin playing.

It made me stand still, like a flower with no wind blowing,
I listen while your words flowed from your sweet lips.
I moved suddenly, like a wind rushing through a forest,
then, I heard your voice saying,
'A woman needs a man for certain things in her life'.
I smiled.

I have always felt strong and independent,
I have always felt no need for a man in my life.
But at that instant, in that very moment,
I felt my body tremble.

Your words railed and twirled, derailing my mind.
It felt like a key fumbling through a locked door,
turning and unlocking the door
that has not seen grease for many years,
bolted closed for too long.

Your voice has found a way to my heart and has entered
where no other could reach for so long.
I felt in my heart you were here to set me free.
My emotions started running inside of me,
and from there on, I cannot stop hearing your voice.

What have you done to me?
Are you an Angel of light?
Are you an Angel of darkness?
I must see you again; I must hear your voice one more time,
for a lifetime.

DOUBTS

Fear is kicking in, my body is shaking.

Doubt is my best friend right now,
your words are tearing at my body.

Being so far away does not help,
water, land, sand and buildings in between us.
People, men and women putting doubts in my mind,
with all these obstacles in our way.

I could and would wait a 100 years for you,
only if doubt could stay out of my mind.

But I am not sure now that you could or would
do the same for me.
I see you baby,
a player.
a sweet talker.
darkness in disguise.

With all doubts I love you,
and I hate you.
You're like a chameleon changing colour,
the only thing is, you're the lizard baby.
I see you slithering and sliding from me to any other
who is foolish enough, to listen to your sweet, false words?

Goodbye doubts,
goodbye fears,
I see you now, your true colours.

HELLO WATER FROM FIRE

Hello water,
I'm fire.
Would you like to try and put me out?

I tell you, you'll have a very hard time doing so,
I don't drown easily!

I rise from below the sea bed,
like a volcano, I lay await till it's my time,
then when I'm above I am curious and hungry.

Wine and dine me.
Place your body over me,
but you will never put me out.
You will caress me; you will be rough with me,

But I'm fire and you can never put me out.
You can try.

Hello water,
I'm willing to let you have a go at trying;
if you succeed then I'm all yours.
But! If you don't succeed you're all mine.
I will burn you from your heart to your mind.

Things that I will do to you... water,
you will want me to keep you flowing and flowing
like a waterfall.
My passion will bring you to the boil
because I am fire.

You cannot drown me; I will not let you,
because I will put a boundary up around you.

I will make a Dam to hold you in
then I will make you boil, and boil,
when you're bubbling and you're so hot
you will know you're on fire,
just like me because I am always hot on fire.

STAND BY EACH OTHER

It is a shame to see that this world, we are living in
Is not really revolving as equals, as partnerships
as women and man together.

There are those of us who see things,
in life that only suits them.
Human beings, I can only laugh at some of the
traits we are born with.

We are more cunning and wicked than
any other creature on this earth.
We effortlessly turn on one another,
instead of standing by each other
unlike the creatures in the wild, we forget to stand by
each other sides, our partner.

I thought we were all equal,
God made woman from the ribs of Adams' side,
So some say!
So then why do we not all walk side by side next to each other,
not in front or behind.

Why then, is it that some men are not equal with their women,
on her vulnerable days? Does love not conquer all things?
All except for God, who put us here for better or worse?
Why are we not standing by each other's side?
Man and woman in every nation.

Man, stand by your woman.
Woman, stand by your man, for better or worse,
especially on the days that she bleeds!
Appreciation is all that she needs.

Will a woman's punishment for Eve's mistake never end?
We bleed once a month, we have labour pain, through childbirth.
Women, we bleed for ourselves, but we also bleed for our men.
So when will man see all women as equal and stand by each other?
Not just the Women with empowered jobs, but all Women.

PIECE OF LAND

From the beginning, the fights have been about the land,
pieces of land that do not belong to any man
but to God alone.
We are the borrowers of this piece of land,
all lands belong to our creator
do you not see that?

Governors, government whatever title you may carry,
do you not see.
You train your soldiers to hate and to fight,
for what reason do they die?
For you or for the land do they fight?
for love, or hate do you train them to kill,
and take for what is not yours,
is this what you command from your soldiers?

Do we not understand?
This piece of land belongs to no one but God,
we are merely just settlers,
looking for a place to rest and be our best,
teach our offspring to love, not fight,
but to make peace not war.

Can we not be left to invent, create
and do our best to stay alive in this world,
on this land we are borrowing?
do we not pay a fortune to stay alive on these borrowed lands
that only belongs to our creator?
In the end, not you, not even I,
will have a say over the piece of land we stand on,
I tell you it belongs to God the creator and only.

TOGETHER WE ARE ONE

Heaven and earth,
two worlds apart
bringing us together.

War let's make peace,
wind blowing my roof around,
thunder blasting over sandy land,
what a combination.

Two people from two different lands
under the same sun,
essence of life pouring over us.

Tree of Life stretching towards the sun
bearing fruits of knowledge,
the magic circle Begins,
together we bonded under its branches.

A hand stretched forth the Holy Grail,
do we dear to take a drink from it?
Temptation wonders through the mind.

The elements are in motion,
emotions are flowing from all Direction,
heaven and earth we are between,
together we are one.

Two people from past and present
neither are alike,
colour we are not the same,
but together we've come,
such beauty as bound us together.
Heaven and earth miracles are performing
as we work together to become one nation.

MY CURIOUS FOOL

You're such a curious fool,
but I'm more curious than you.

I don't judge you,
I will never hate you,
I cannot wait to look into your eyes
and see right through your soul.

I cannot wait to make love to you.
Not sex, but make love to you
my curious fool.
You and I together are breathless.

I don't hate you, nor will I ever.
Sometimes I want to run away from you
and hide for a while,
but you call me and I hear it in your voice,
you're curious, you're missing me.

I remember your dreamy eyes undressing me,
I remember your tongue washing over me
like a damp cloth wiping over my body,
now I'm back to being curious.

Wanting more of you,
I cannot wait to make love to you.
Not sex, but make love to you.
I'm coming home my curious fool
to fall asleep in your arms.

I HAD A DREAM

I dreamt Cupid and Aphrodite's are having a fight.
War between two lovers,
well, where does that leave us, mankind?
Cupid is supposed to draw the arrow
that shoots between you and me,
to join us together as one.

In my dream Aphrodite's she kisses me on my cheek,
then she kisses you on your cheek.
She blows the breath of love into our hearts
so for us to fall in love.

Now Aphrodite's and Cupid are at war with each other.
Where does that leave us?
Does that mean true love is gone?
Love, just like that out the window.

No wonder man, woman and children, everyone
different colours, different races,
same race, same colour all in war with one another.
Who's going to put the peace
between Aphrodite's and Cupid back together?
If they can't find peace, we're doomed.
Find the timepiece and the peacemaker.
Who has it?

My dream is vanishing away.
Before I leave, who's the strongest amongst us
that dares come between Aphrodite's and Cupid?
Stop their war someone, and maybe there will be
hope for our war to be stopped.

I hope they find the strongest amongst themselves
before it's too late for us all.
Find the timekeeper and the peacemaker.
Who has the power?
Hurry, put a stop to my dream, and wake me up.
Love cannot die for Cupid and Aphrodite's.

MINDFUL

Where are my features?
what are my benefits?
Why are you stopping me from reaching my destination?
Why is there a big objection coming from you
every time I open my mouth?
I just want to tell you what I am aiming for in this life.

We are business-minded, playful-minded.
But I can see the difference,
it's written all over your face,
I can feel it burning through my soul,
we are so different.

There is never any support from you,
I can see now my mind and yours
are so different from each other.
We are both business-minded people.
You don't like to play a little outside your box,
I'm like a kitten hard at work,
yet I like to play in my spare time.

Baby you wrap yourself up in a blanket,
TV on, fingers going fast as lightning.
Head spaced out playing your video games.
But me, I want to play a different kind of game.

Maybe it is time for us to say goodbye.
Now is the right time while we can still talk to one another.
If we wait till later only God knows
what will happen by then.
I can see now you're hurting and I am hurting too,
we are both so much alike, yet so different.

We are business-minded, playful-minded.
But I can see the difference.
It's written all over your face
I can feel it burning through my soul,
we are so different.

LOVE IS A BEAUTIFUL THING

Love is a beautiful thing.
Can you feel it?
Do you feel it?

I travel down the highway creating thoughts in my mind,
it's beautiful what I see.
My imagination of Angels spreading their wings across the sky,
the feelings that I feel, is of love, so far and wide.

Like the wings of an Angel gliding through the wind
over and above mountains.
When we're together life is so different,
my imaginations far and few flying away on an Angel's back
life is, so beautiful.
Now is the time for only truth,
now is the time to believe, the time is ripe for us.

Love is a beautiful thing.
Can you feel it?
Do you feel it?

Like the wings of angels gliding through the wind,
see how low they fly.
Touching the top of the sea with their wings,
gliding upwards,
vanishing in the glare of the sun.
Life is so beautiful.

I travel down the highway creating thoughts in my mind,
it's beautiful what I see.
Angel wings gliding through and over trees, water and land
vanishing in the clouds overhead it seems.
Love is a beautiful thing, when we carry it in our heart.
Can you feel it?
Do you feel it?

ANOTHER LAND

How life must feel as a child.
Watching your mother and father,
handing over their life savings to strangers,
on the edge of a seashore.
Hoping to find another land safer than this one,
you're leaving behind.
You and your siblings getting on a boat with strangers,
knowing not how strange the next atmosphere will be for you
or your family in another land.

In the boat, on the sea, going over rough waters,
vomiting screaming babies, adults old and young,
conscious scared wondering where, when their journey will end.
What will be waiting for them? Freedom is their hope!
Praying in their hearts they will find kindness, in another land.

Hearts that will open up and accept them with kindness
Is there hope, waiting for them somewhere,
on another land in this world?
Still, they are fearful in their hearts, of the not known.
People that would not understand them,
or where they are coming from.

Rough waters! Boats rocking one side to another riding the
waves, some boats turning over, upside down.
Screaming shouting, voices gulping water in their chest
and stomach, survivors watching bodies floating around them,
some watching their own family, and friends floating around,
trying their hardest to hold on to them, too late they are gone.

The water is cold their bodies are cold, what disaster,
what an abomination brave and yet frighten scared.
Oh my Lord. They reach their destination another land.
Not all are so lucky; some are treated like animals with fleas
some are worse. It is hard to imagine this is another land,
the lucky ones will find another land of freedom,
another home, where you and I are. A land of reason!
A land of hope!

A QUESTION OF GOD

This question has been asked
over and over again,
but, I really don't think
anyone has the answer to it.

What is God?
Who is God Really?
Is God a woman or a man?

Does anyone have the faintest idea?

My belief;
God is my belief,
God is here and everywhere.

God is in the child that suffers,
God is in the woman, man begging on the streets,
God is in the old and the young suffering with aches pains, illness,
God is in the powerful that speaks the truth,
God is nowhere, yet everywhere.
In the air around us that we breathe in,
in every sip of the water we drink,
in the earth we walk upon,
in the true fire that keeps us warm.

So who is God?
What is God?
God is whoever, whatever you believe in.
I cannot tell you, nor can I judge your belief,
nor none should judge you, but God!
your believe.

I will say my believing of God is that.
When we believe in God then God lives in our heart.
God is everything we See, Feel, Taste and Love or even dislike.
But most of all,
God is the greatest of all love that is known,
God is known by so many names.
That is my belief.

CRAZY MYSTICAL

I am going crazy mystical,
I am burning brighter than ever before
as my aura shines.
The sun has changed, I am stronger,
I've drawn its power.

I am going crazy mystical for love,
tonight the moon has changed,
I can feel her/him, the mystical power,
of the paled veiled face running through my veins.

The moon as turned red,
my blood is boiling in my body,
from the power of the sun,
I can feel my temperature rising and boiling.
This mystical feeling is sending me crazy.

Hearing the sound of water from far,
I look up and it's raining showering my face,
cooling my body.
Beyond the drops of water upon my face
I gazed upon the stars above.

Through the dark sky the stars shines,
one, two stars falling, orange, yellow and red
burning through the sky.
Star fire does not fear me,
I am going crazy mystical for love.

I am fire itself, I'm mystical.
I am burning out of control for affection,
the sun has changed, I'm stronger,
I've drawn its mystical power.

I am going crazy mystical for love.
Who dares to put this fire out inside of me?
Crazy mystical is what you will find.

IF I TRY MY HARDEST

If I try my hardest, will you bring peace to this land?
You gave me a dream, a vision of fantasy that may never be seen,
I have been your Seer for such a long time.
I've seen war; I've seen so many lovers come together,
Just, to fall apart.

I have been one of those that has fallen in love
and fallen out of love, so many times.
Now this is my last time for love.
If I try my hardest and give thee the gift of love
give thee the gift of my soul.
Will you bring peace to this land?

I read the latest news this morning,
the war brings tears to my eyes again,
it literally made me scream for Peace.
I wish I could hold my love ones tight in my arms, and
make them feel secure a little longer.

I have called upon the fire to bring light and it did.
I have called upon the water to rain, rain came.
I called upon the wind to carry my spirit afar and it did so.
When I asked the earth to move my garden around, it also did.
But I cannot stop the wars.

When is it going to end? I have been your Seer for such a long time.
When is our Almighty going to answer our prayers?
and stop the children, the old and the young from
suffering from these conflicted, lust and hunger.

Has our creator abandoned us?
I have not been to many parts of the world,
yet I seek peace for the world.
My soul belongs to you, but! My heart belongs to the world
I am a seer of yours.

So if I try my hardest, will you bring peace.
I have been a seer for such a long time,
Peace please I seek.

HEAR MY VOICE

I am a damsel in distress, carrying a heavy load of past mistakes,
looking for somewhere to unload my misery.
I have been wicked, I am a sinner in distress.
I sit with my legs crossed on the green grass,
listening to the birds, watching the white butterfly,
hovering over above my body.

I look up to the sky, so clear and blue it is.
I close my eyes, feeling the warmth of the sun upon my face.
Through my face, I feel my body on fire.
I'm meditating, I pray as I meditate that my voice,
the inner voice will be acceptable, when the wind carries
it through the air, along to that mystical forest
of waterfalls, rainbows without rain falling, just vapour of rain.

I am hoping that I am strong enough to accept
the knowledge that will befall upon me.
I now entwine myself with the universe to be strong enough
for my inner person to be heard.

Here I am in silence, trying so hard to purify myself
once more the sun pours its sacred fire down on me.
I seek its fire to purify my soul. my imagination gazes through
my closed eyes up to the clear blue sky through my mind,
to escape from my sins.

I pray that while I meditate
my voice will be carried through the universe,
that my meditation will be accepted, with wide arms open for me.
As my inner body leave this mystical forest of waterfalls,
rainbows and vapour of rain.
I watch the clear blue sky along with its white patches of clouds,
sending their messages to me.

My mind is now full of knowledge,
I know now my meditation; my voice has been heard
and accepted. I have been cleansed.
Blessed be Alpha and Omega.
The beginning and the end.

THE RAIN

Tip, tap, drizzling, drop and down I go,
I can come slow, fast, or heavy,
yet so fine at times.

It's no one's choice,
it's no one's but mine
how I come,
how I present myself to you.

I am from a heavenly place,
far from no human beings.
Woo, how fine it feels to land on a tree full of leaves.

I can run down each leaf slowly,
down the bark I flow to the trunk of the tree,
until I get to the ground and work my way through to the soil.

I am a great part of survival for everything and everyone.
I dissolve to nothing yet heavenly goodness.

I give man and all creatures' life,
I nourish the land,
enrich the soil and clear the air,
For a smile to some but not to all,
I am rain.

DREAM WONDERING MIND

The wind with its powerful grace
meets me at the door as I open it.
It feels strong, it blows me with aggressiveness,
I feel I should step back indoors and close the door.

But my sixth sense says different.
Walk out and embrace the wind,
whatever follows, will follow gracefully.
The elements are strong but they need you.
I can feel them overpowering me,
But! I know if I place my mind in the elements,
they will carry me away and I will feel their acceptance.

I walk in the garden slowly.
As my mind wondered my body and legs take
step after step until I reached the garden wall.
I sit on the wall with my eyes closed.
I feel the warmth of the sun around me,
it embraces me with a mighty feeling of power.
Both my feet flat to the ground, feeling the earth
beneath them accepting me.

Again, I can feel the anger of the wind
surrounding me, almost knocking me off the wall.
The sound of anger, almost like a roaring lion
with a tinch of the sound of the sea in its roaring.

I sat and wrote.
The wind calmed itself around me a few times,
then got angry again,
showing me its strength.
I got up and walked back to the house
and opened the door.
As I walked in the house,
the door slammed behind me.
I jumped from my sleep and realised
it was all a dream.

THE EYES OF AN EAGLE

From up here,
I see the beauty and mystery of my world.
I am away from the war below.

Soon I will be tired of flying and need to rest
my wings, among the fighting below.

I pray and hope I find a place of peace,
where my landing will not be a hunting ground.
I hope for a place on the ground to set my soul
and rest my wings for a while.

Freedom I long for,
don't judge me because I have wings.
You may think because I am an Eagle, I should be a free bird.
But mankind has many cages,
I seek the higher wind for freedom,
yet the needs fall upon me for a place to rest on the ground.

I pray and hope I find a place of peace
where my landing will not be a hunting ground,
to set my soul and rest my wings
for a while.

When I land, I should land safely,
peace is what I seek
but war is what I might find below.

HE CAUGHT MY ATTENTION

I saw a young man walking past me yesterday,
He caught my attention while I sat waiting for my friend.
The young man walked so tall,
he walked with grace written all over his face.

Even though he was not very tall,
he walked with style but was not dressed with style.
His attention was looking straight ahead
while he walked on by, but still,
he caught my attention.

I wished I could walk as confident as he did.
I wished I had stopped him and talked to him,
while I sat waiting for my friend.

So many other people walked on by,
but only he stood out of the crowd.
I remember clearly what he was wearing,
striped pullover, a pair of jeans
and a cigarette in his hand, smoking.
He defiantly caught my attention.

I never clearly saw his face.
I don't even remember the colour of his shoes,
neither do I remember the colour of his hair,
only that his hair was dark.
I also remembered the way he walked,
he stood out from the crowd
and caught my attention.

THE INNOCENTS

Stand and guard the innocents!
from this hollow and shattered world,
It will feed upon the innocents.

Let's cast out the darkness
dance, with and through the light,
Upset not our creator,
the possessed, and emptiness as found us,
the innocent ones.

What will you miss?
Can there be life after this?
So much blank space, massacre of lives,
man, woman and children slaughtered for what?

A piece of land that belongs to no man,
whether win or lose,
in the end only the innocent loses.
The rich and powerful feeds upon the innocents' mind
draw their ideas and strength,
for their own rewards.

We don't belong here, too much darkness,
too much massacre of the innocent,
man woman and children,
all in the name of the powerful man
or woman that governs the land.

Let's dance with and through the light,
In the end only the innocent loses,
only the innocent are sent to fight
and once again the govern hides.

DARKNESS INSIDE ME

Wake up. Wake up! You must go now.
Go before the demon rises inside of me.
We had a wonderful night, it was beautiful,
I loved the way we moved.
Motions flowing from each other's body
moving with rhythms.

But now the sun is rising
the darkness is moving inside of me,
I fear I feel no control to save you if it finds
you here next to me.

Wake up I urge you.
Make haste, leave now, think not of me.
We were sweet and passionate.
We were pure together, not so now.
I am not bitter but the darkness lives inside of me,
it watches for any mate I may take,
it will devour you if it finds you lying beside me.

Wake up you must go before sunrise.
I see the sun and I feel the darkness, it is fighting its way through,
I want you to stay, but I need you to go.
I want to feel your closeness beside me, but I need you to leave.
Leave now, far away from beside me.
I need you to run for your life,
yet I want your touch when I awaken,
but up you must get and flee for your life.

The Darkness is rising inside of me,
good or bad I know not if we will meet again.
I don't know if we will make love again. I don't know...
I hope for this motion to be set in a different direction,
should we meet again, I pray for it to be so.

Will we have this circle again?
I know nothing; the Darkness is here inside of me,
It keeps me as its bond slave.
So wake up, go now, as I'm able to set you free my sweetness.

THINGS ON MY MIND

There are things on my mind,
things that I cannot explain.
I am feeling confused, things happening around me,
strange things.

There are things in my head trying to get out,
I cannot explain them.
They say they are from that mystical place
mankind is looking for.
We were full of oh, oh.
Wow, that is so strange.

I feel like I'm floating on air,
yet I feel like I'm drowning at the same time.
Mystical, mystical feelings burning away at me,
At the same time emptiness, empty feelings,
things on my mind no escape.

It is as if I can smell something in the air is coming.
I cannot explain these feelings,
but something is coming.
My body tingles. It warns me of danger.

My head is feeling very strange, things on my mind
make my eyes not wanting to see things of this world anymore.
Words are coming out of my mouth, yet it is not I
that is saying these things.

Time is running out, emptiness is coming
I can feel it,
It makes me feel like I'm flying in fear.
Its closeness is coming, it is here.
Doomsday emptiness is here.
But there are things on my mind I wish I could have told you before this day.
But confused I was and still I am.

SWEET LOVE

Whenever you take me in your arms
and make love to me, it is sweet love.
I taste your sweat as it pours from your soul
through to the surface of your outer skin,
covering your whole body.

When you put your arms around me,
It makes me feel like the sea caressing my body,
you are the waves drowning me.
When the sweat falls from your body it is your sweet love
unto my naked body that it falls,
It takes my thoughts to the waves of the sea
crashing against the rocks.

When we kiss my sweet love, my teeth gip your bottom lip,
It's like sucking on a sweet cherry,
firm but yet soft, smooth and so sweet,
with a little taste of salt, like the sea water.

When you place your head on my bosom
I feel like I have found the child within you,
that has been looking for comfort from my love.
So I gladly give comfort with love to you.

When we sleep in closeness together
we entwine in love around each other,
with sweat pouring from each other, in the mist of the night,
There is no other love that can be as close as ours,
It makes me feel like the sea caressing my body,
you are the waves that I see drowning me, yet caressing me
with love and care,
You are my sweet love.

I SEE YOU IN MY DREAMS

As I sit among the trees.
I become drowsy,
half asleep and half awake.

I am sure, I see you walking towards me.
Your shirt fully buttoned.

The closer you get to me, the buttons on your shirt,
you're ripping them apart,
your shirt is wide open now,
revealing your chest to me.
You run your fingers through your black-grey flecks of hair.

There's a slight breeze that catches the shirt
to make it flap and flap,
as you move faster towards me.

As you become closer and closer to me,
I can almost feel you touching me.

Suddenly I can feel the thrust of your arms
pushing me to the ground.
Your lips smack against mine.

Gentle in your ears I whisper,
"How sweet it is to see you,
to see you baby."

You hold me tight,
Then! You pull my thighs up from being flat on the ground.
Gently you rub your hands up and down,
evenly over my thighs,
I whisper in your ear again, "Perfect my Prince,
I see you baby."

HAS YOUR PERCEPTION OF ME CHANGED?

Has your perception of me changed?
Over the years and months, of knowing me,
If so, please don't be afraid to tell me.
Delicate I may seem, but my strength lies within me,

I had an idea the other day,
and would you believe it.
It was a leaf flying by in the wind
that brought my mind to this matter.
Has the conversation we had the other day
changed your perception of me?

Everything inside me is saying that I am human
yet still there is something telling me different.
Right now this feeling is driving me crazy.
Voices screaming at me, reminding me
that I have told you who I am, where I am from.
We spoke of many different things,
different nationalities, different colours, races even Aliens.
So now tell me,
has your perception of me changed?

My heart is racing like mad,
I can feel my blood racing through my veins.
It's like watching water running from a tap,
you are not human.
The voices again over and over in my head,
my heart is telling me they are right.

So now I ask have you, one more time.
Has your perception of me changed?
over the years and months, of knowing me.

IS MY CHILD NOT MY CHILD?

I know this child I carry inside me is not like my others.
This child is mine, yet this child is not mine.
This child belongs to no man on this planet.

This child belongs nowhere,
yet he or she belongs everywhere.
Do you ask if the Messiah has returned again?
Do you ask is my child not my child.

No, but yes, yes but no,
a blessing will come forth
a blessing will be Reborn,
the light and darkness shall come together.

Where men could not bring peace,
joy and laughter shall be heard.
There shall be peace seen on faces of old young sick and the poor.

This child shall move mountains,
 that man has been struggling with for centuries.
This child shall make miracles happen.
This child shall speak all tongues of this world.

This child is mine, but yet he or she is not mine,
he or she belongs everywhere,
yet nowhere in this world.

Should the father of this child know of this child's existence?
Should the mother keep this child's identity between herself?
the universe, the creator,
that made it possible again?
So must it be.

THE WIND

My oh my,
you are a teaser.
Oh you are.

You come from so many different directions,
North, South, East and the West,
you come on so strong around me.

You blow my mind away,
like you do with the leaves dancing in your spell.
You can be so cold,
yet you're so warm when you want to be.

My oh my,
You are a teaser, just look at the way
you play with my clothes hanging from my clothesline,
Oh, you are such a teaser.

Coming from the North, South, East and West
You can be so good to me,
yet you're so rough at times you are a teaser.

Breaking things outside rustling, crushing things like trees,
Angry one minute, calm the next,
then you blow my mind away,
You are definitely my wild wind.

AFTERMATH

This is the aftermath of a war.
People wandering around,
complicated complications,
written all over their faces.

Their aftermath of waking up after the bombing,
one arm, no arms,
one leg, no legs,
one eye, no eyes.

Blood and bodies everywhere,
children, babies, women and man groaning and crying.

The young and the old,
searching for their loved ones,
through rubble,
looking for a sense of direction.
Where to start?

Whether to continue fighting for life,
or maybe, pick up the gun at his or her feet,
run, charging at the ones,
that are aiming their guns at them,
hoping for a quick death!
In the head nothing making any sense.

Was any of this worth the lifeless bodies lying at their feet?
Where are their loved ones?
Are they dead or alive?
How many bodies do they need to step over?
To find the one they are looking for.
Will he or she ever find that person alive or dead?
This is the aftermath of being at the end of a war.

FRIENDS

Friends, we are strength together!
We give to one another, support!
Praise each other to be confident,
the further we go into the future
we vow!
To fight every step of the way together,
side by side!
With each other's words of empowerment!
Let our words be our sword, my friends,
until we meet again, champions and friends we are!

VENGEANCE!

Today is the day we seek Vengeance!
for our mother and father.
We were only two years old
when they came into our home,

Broke the door down,
pushed us aside like rag dolls.
They thought we were dead,
because they had banged our heads together,
knocked us down to the ground,
out like lightning.
They left us for dead they thought we were!

We went into darkness for a while.
Thank the lord we stayed unconscious till they left!
But! now we are old enough to seek vengeance
for our mother and father.
We are in training our blood runs on fire for vengeance,

On our knees, we bent in prayer for years seeking
revenge of our parents. Stop our boiling blood,
show them we are strong!
Revengeance is not ours to take, pardon them we must.
Revenge we have found through hope and faith in our hearts.

FORGIVENESS

I'm surprised I'm still standing here.
Been down these roads so many times,
done with all these talks of forgetting.
I've forgiven, but can never forget!

Whoever says forgive and forget?
Such stupid words,
you can forgive.
but! you can never nor should you ever forget!

I have forgiven a lot in my lifetime,
time to move on.
Let's not forget a lesson learned,
What has been said and done
let's put to rest, so I have heard.

Forgiving is a way of learning!
you're learning to trust as life goes on,
who or what to give a little leeway to,
who not to give any more to,
who to give that big trust back to.

Forgiveness is a great gift!
but not forgetting is a greater gift!
or else, so many of us would be hurt
over and over again, or be killed eventually.
You forgot that darkness can rise within trusting,
and lead you down that wrong path as before.

Forgiving means you can walk away
with what you have learned, never come back.
If you come back, you come back with knowledge!
You should be wiser, know how to trust
and how much trust to give again.

Forgiveness is a great gift!
Forgiveness is a great way of learning,
but never forgetting is a greater gift!

YOU'RE HOVERING!

You hover over me everywhere I go,
your shadow hovers over me.
Where ever I am and I hear a familiar voice,
turn around and your shadow is right there in my face.

I opened the front door.
The first thing I hear is your voice.
My body moves and turns around the house,
to enter each and every room.

I turn around and oh my gosh,
it is you! That is right there, standing over me hovering!
Again, nagging, annoying,
always having something to say.

It is then I say, "Oh I wish I didn't need to come home.
I wish I could get away from you for a while", so much hovering.
Why are you always here?
In my face,
your body, your voice the first thing in the morning,
last thing at night, how annoying.

Now you're gone I'll never see that face again.
I'll never see that body again,
I'll never hear that voice again.
I am surrounded by friends' family and so many beautiful people.

Yet, all I can think of!
Yes, I wish you were here hovering over me right now.
I wish you were the first thing I see when I walk in the door.
I wish I could hear that annoying voice of yours,
asking me this and that,
telling me all you did and did not do,
during those few hours of being apart,
Oh, I miss your hovering over me!

CONFUSION

Hello my universe, my creatures,
I am confused?
Tell me, can a wolf howl as I do?
for the one that I love so dearly.

Can a horse run as fast as my heart beats?
with the pain, confusion and sorrow that I feel for
the one that I love.
My body quivers like a woman giving birth to a child.

I feel like a spear has just been pierced
through my side, as did with Jesus Christ.
I feel like my heart has been ripped out of my chest,
like a vampire taking its prey for joy.

I feel like I have no life left inside of me.
I cried every night and day,
like a banshee, I scream out your name from my sleep,
the pain still aches, it confuses my mind.
How can love be so sweet, and yet so bitter, cruel?
I am so confused.

How can love be so good, and yet hurts so badly?
My heart as no place in this body no more.
It is like looking into a cracked mirror and
If you try to embrace me, I would surely shatter to pieces.

Your love as left me in torment, agony,
that's my heart now confused.

SPRITE OF MY LIFE

You are the sprite in my life honey.
Summer comes summer goes but you stay,
you season up my life, the entire time baby.

You put me on a stage, without you knowing.
I like a sip of port now and again,
but when you're around me, or I hear your voice,
I need no Port.
You make me feel so proud to be with you.

Baby, maybe I'm crazy, for telling you these things,
for undoubtedly, your words touch my heart,
you sprite up my life all the time.

You are the sprite in my life honey.
Summer comes summer goes but you stay,
you season up my life, the entire time baby.

I can feel the branches of your heart reaching out to me,
Unnameable I question not my feelings of your worth to me.
Now that I really know you are worthy, of my love,
oh baby, baby.

You are the sprite in my life honey.
Summer comes summer goes.
But you season up my life the entire time baby.

You make me feel so proud, so, so proud.
Maybe I'm crazy, for telling you these things,
but you're the sprite,
you are the sprite in my life.

HAVE A LITTLE FAITH

When your body has become numb,
your ears have become so confused,
you cannot hear me speaking to you.
My sweetness, remember my voice.
Have a little faith!

Know my heart!
Know my voice!
Don't let your tears blind you.

When life becomes like champagne bubbles,
popping out of control.
Slow down sweetness.
Have a little faith!

Champagne bubbles rise and dance,
like crazy till pop at top of glass.
Slow down take a deep breath.

Stand fast,
be still in faith.
Have a little faith.
Reach out to me!

Pamper your heart.
Spoil your mind,
see life for what it is.
Like a baby bird fallen from its nest,
helpless but not hopeless it lies await.

Mama will surely come to pick me up,
it tweets.

Through the wind I will hear your heart beat,
hear your whispering words riding the wind,
I will be there.
Just have a little faith in me!

STOP BLINDING YOUR EYES FROM ME

Stop blinding your eyes from me.
Stop turning your ears from me.
Stop making me think that you do not understand me anymore.

Know that I am here!
Know that I have been asking, begging, preaching and praying
for you,
for your understanding,
for your help, for your attention,
for your knowledge, your love
and peace.

Stop blinding your eyes from me.
Stop turning your ears from me.
Stop making me think that you do not understand me anymore.

My knees are bent,
my hands are stretched out to you,
my eyes are closed,
Reach down and touch me on my shoulder, I beg you.
Stop turning your ears from me.

Touch me like you did the day I was filled with your spirit.
Reach out once more and let me know your presence is still
within me.
You sent an Angel to watch over me,
I do not feel that presence at this moment.

Please?
Stop blinding your eyes from me.
Stop turning your ears from me.
Stop making me think that you do not understand me anymore.

www.ingramcontent.com/pod-product-compliance
Lightning Source LLC
Chambersburg PA
CBHW050321010526
44107CB00055B/2340